EXPOSITION

OF THE

CLAIM OF G. A. LeMORE & CO.,

TO

EIGHT HUNDRED AND THIRTY BALES OF COTTON DETAINED BY THE UNITED STATES AS PRIZE OF WAR.

By JOHN A. McCLERNAND.

McGill & Witherow, Printers & Stereotypers, Washington. D.C.

EXPOSITION

OF THE CLAIM OF G. A. LEMORE & CO. TO EIGHT HUNDRED AND THIRTY BALES OF COTTON DETAINED BY THE UNITED STATES AS PRIZE OF WAR.

BY JOHN A. McCLERNAND.

FACTS.

Gustave A. LeMore and Leontine LeMore, citizens of France, composing the firm of G. A. LeMore & Co., of Havre, on the first of March, A. D. 1864, by their agent, Jules LeMore, also a French citizen, purchased of Leon Quegrouze, a naturalized citizen of the United States, within a district of Louisiana then, *in fact*, under the military and civil jurisdiction of the revolutionary government of the Confederate States of America, eight hundred and thirty bales of cotton. For these cottons, LeMore & Co. paid $160 per bale, actually took possession of them, (by their agent,) and without delay removed them to the bank of the Ouachita river, within the same jurisdiction. Here, while their agent was marking them with the initials of his principals, preparatory to shipment, they were seized by the United States Navy as prize of war. Subsequently, the cottons were carried to Cairo and libelled in the United States court, of the southern district of Illinois, and sold under an interlocutory decree as perishable property; the proceeds of which sale, still in the hands of the court, remain to be disposed of.

LeMore & Co., having filed their answer to the libel, praying restitution of the cottons, and denying that they are lawful prize, the cause came on to be heard, and the court made an order dismissing their claim, but left the question of prize and confiscation undetermined. From that order, LeMore & Co. have appealed to the Supreme Court of the United States, and it now remains for that Court, in the ordinary course of procedure, either to affirm the order and condemn the goods as lawful prize, or to disaffirm it, and distribute the funds according to right among the claimants, or to disaffirm it, and remand the cause and direct the court below to make such distribution.

LAW OF THE CASE.

The character of the late war in the United States must be considered in determining the legal principles by which this cause must be governed. The war was a domestic one, and had been prosecuted for the full period of four years when these cottons were seized. Meantime, eleven States, extending from the Potomac more than three thousand miles along the Atlantic coast to the Rio Grande, had formally seceded from the American Union. These States embraced an area of 707,548 square miles, a population of 9,103,383 souls, and were many times larger in extent than the empire of France. After having seceded, they formed a distinct confederation and instituted an elective government, which passed laws, administered public justice, raised and supported armies, appointed foreign ministers, and exercised all the sovereignty, and performed all the acts, common to free and independent governments.

The people of these States arrayed themselves in hostility to the old Union, and marshaled hosts for the purpose of gaining their independence. Millions of combatants on one side and the other were brought into the field, and fought over an extended empire, with alternating success, the most sanguinary battles known to modern times. Several of these battles occurred near the Federal capital, and one of the most important of them in a loyal State. Two hundred and seventy five vessels, public and private, sailing under Federal colors, were captured by Confederate privateers, and probably a million of men perished in the field, in hospitals, and otherwise, as a consequence of the war. The debt entailed by it on the Federal Government must amount to some four thousand millions of dollars, and that incurred on on the other side is quite as large. The Confederates, although not recognized by foreign governments as an independent nation, were nevertheless recognized by France,

England, and Spain, as a belligerent power; entitled as such to all the rights accorded to its adversary.

Was this war an insurrection or a rebellion, amenable as a state crime to the municipal law? It would be an abuse of terms to say so. It was a war falling essentially within the reason and definition of a *civil war*, and as such must, as to both the belligerents and to neutral nations, be viewed in the light of the public law, as applicable to foreign belligerent States. The same laws are applicable to the one as to the other.

France, England, and Spain have so declared, by recognizing the Confederates as a belligerent power.

Publicists, in treating of the qualities of such a war, and of the legal relations growing out of it, lay it down that, "war between the different members of the same society is a" "civil" or "mixed war," but the general usage of nations regards such a war as entitling both of the contending parties to all the rights of war as against each other, and even as respects neutral nations." (Grotius, de jur., Bel. ac Pac., lib. 3, chap. 9, sec. 3; Rutherford's Inst., b. 2, c. 10, sec. 12, 13; Lawrence's Wheaton on Intern. Law, Part 4, chap. 1, pp. 522, 3.)

Again, "a civil war is where a party arises in a State which no longer obeys the sovereign, and is sufficiently strong to make head against him, or when, in a republic, the nation is divided into two opposite factions, and both sides take up arms. It is sufficient that the malcontents have some reason to take up arms, in order that the disturbances should be called *civil war*, and not *rebellion*."

The prince never fails to call rebels all his subjects who openly resist him; but when the latter become sufficiently strong to make head against him, to compel him to carry on war regularly against them, he must be contented with the term "*civil war*."

Civil war breaks the bonds of society and of the government; it gives rise in a nation to two independent parties, who acknowledge no common judge. They are in the position of two nations who engage in disputes, and not being able to reconcile them, have recourse to arms. The common laws of war are in civil wars to be observed on both sides. The same reasons which make them obligatory between foreign States, render them more necessary in the unhappy circumstances where two exasperated parties are destroying their common country.

If the sovereign considers himself authorized to hang

prisoners as rebels, the opposite party will have recourse to reprisals; if he burns and devastates, they will do the same; war will become cruel, terrible, and always more destructive to the nation.

When a nation becomes divided into two parties absolutely independent, and no longer acknowledging a common superior, the State is dissolved, and the war betwixt the two parties, in every respect, is the same as that of a public war between different nations. The obligation of observing the common law of war, is, therefore, absolutely indispensable to both parties, and the same which the law of nature obliges all nations to observe between State and State." (Vattel, Droit des Gens, liv. 3, chap. 18, sec. 290–295.)

Riguelme says: "As true civil war breaks the bonds of society by dividing it, in fact, into two independent societies, it is for this consideration that we treat of it in international law; since each party forms, as it were, a separate nation, both should be regarded as subject to the laws of war." (Elementos de Derecho Publico, cap. 14, tom. 1, p. 172.)

Bello says: "When a faction is formed in a State, which takes up arms against the sovereign, in order to wrest from him the supreme power, or impose conditions on him; or when a republic is divided into two parties, which mutually treat each other as enemies, this war is called *civil war*, which means war between fellow-citizens.

"Civil wars frequently commenced by popular tumults, which in nowise concern foreign nations; but when one faction or party obtains dominion over an extensive territory, gives laws to it, establishes a government in it, administers justice, and, in a word, exercises acts of sovereignty, *it is a person in the law of nations;* and however so much one of the two parties gives to the other the title of rebel or tyrant, the foreign powers which desire to maintain their neutrality ought to consider both as two States, independent as respects one another and other States, and who recognize no judge of their differences." (Principios de Derecho Internacional, cap. 10, p. 267.)

This recital of these facts and authorities establishes two positions: 1st. That the belligerent parties in the late civil war in America were, as to each other and to foreign powers, in contemplation of the public law, independent nations. 2d. That their rights and responsibilities, as belligerents, relatively to each other, and to neutral nations, and of the latter to the former, are fixed and determined by that law, and are the same applicable to belligerent foreign powers.

In other words, that the rule of reciprocity, fundamental in the law of nations, obtains in this case, according to the relations of the different parties to each other.

The question now arises, what were the commercial relations and rights existing between the Federalists and Confederates, respectively, as belligerent powers, and the French empire and its citizens as a neutral nation? Clearly, the same rights existed between either of these belligerents and France. If LeMore & Co., as neutrals, had the right to trade with the Federalists, they had an equal right to trade with the Confederates. Had they the right to trade with either? The answer to this question turns, *first*, on the nationality of these parties, which is conclusively proven to have been French, not only by their nativity, but by their actual residence at the date of their purchase of these cottons. *Secondly*, as Frenchmen and neutrals, were they authorized by the law of nations to make the particular purchase?

Wheaton says: "The primitive law, independently of international compact, rests on the simple principle, that war gives a right to capture the goods of an enemy, but gives no right to capture the goods of a friend. The exemption on neutral property from capture has *no other exceptions* than those arising from the carrying of contraband, breach of blockade, and other analogous cases, where the conduct of the neutral gives to the belligerent a right to treat his property as enemy's property." (Lawrence's Wheaton, Part IV, ch. 3, p. 739.)

"The public law of Europe has established the principle, that, in time of war, countries no parties to the war, nor interposing in it, shall not be materially affected by its action; but they shall be permitted to carry out their accustomed trade, under the few necessary restrictions which we shall hereafter consider." (Kent's Com's, vol. 1, p. 124, 10th edition.)

These restrictions are those above enumerated.

Now, it is not pretended that these cottons were contraband of war, or were in any way obnoxious to the law of blockade; and, if it were so pretended, it would be in the face of all reason and all facts. On the contrary, they stand as lawful goods, upon the recognized and solid foundations of lawful neutral trade.

It is objected, however, that they are obnoxious to the operation of certain municipal statutes and proclamations.

How so? The first of these statutes is entitled "An Act

to provide for the collection of duties on imports, and for other purposes," approved July 13, 1861, and provides in the fifth section,

"That whenever the President, in pursuance of the provisions of the second section of the act, entitled 'An Act to provide for calling forth the militia to execute the laws of the Union, suppress insurrections, and repel invasions, and to repeal the act now in force for that purpose,' approved February 28, 1795, shall have called forth the militia to suppress combinations against the laws of the United States, and to cause the laws to be duly executed, and the insurgents shall have failed to disperse by the time directed by the President, and when said insurgents claim to act under the authority of any State or States, and such claim is not disclaimed or repudiated by the persons exercising the functions of government in such State or States, or in the parts thereof in which said combination exists, nor such insurrection suppressed by such State or States, then, and in such case, it may and shall be lawful for the President, by proclamation, to declare that the inhabitants of such State, or any section or part thereof, where such insurrection exists, are in a state of insurrection against the United States; and thereupon all commercial intercourse by and between the same, and the citizens thereof and the citizens of the rest of the United States, shall cease and be unlawful, so long as such condition of hostility shall continue; and all goods and chattels, wares and merchandise, coming from said State or section into the other parts of the United States, and all proceeding to such State or section by land or water, shall, together with the vessel or vehicle conveying the same, or conveying persons to or from such State or section, be forfeited to the United States: *Provided, however*, That the President may, in his discretion, license or permit commercial intercourse with any such part of said State or section, the inhabitants of which are so declared in a state of insurrection, in such articles, and for such time, and by such persons, as he, in his discretion, may think most conducive to the public interest; and such intercourse, so far as by him licensed, shall be conducted and carried on only in pursuance of rules and regulations prescribed by the Secretary of the Treasury. And the Secretary of the Treasury may appoint such officers, at places where officers of the customs are not now authorized by law, as may be needed to carry into effect such licenses, rules, and regulations," &c. (United States Stats. at Large, vol. 12, p. 257.)

The proclamation made by the President pursuant to this act is in material part as follows:

"Now, therefore, I, Abraham Lincoln, President of the United States, * * do hereby declare, that the inhabitants of the said States of Georgia, South Carolina, Virginia, North Carolina, Tennessee, Alabama, Louisiana, Texas, Arkansas, Mississippi, and Florida, excepting certain loyal parts of disloyal States and their inhabitants, and such other parts of such States that may become occupied and controlled by the forces of the United States, are in a state of insurrection against the United States; and that all commercial intercourse between the same and the inhabitants thereof, with the exceptions aforesaid, and the citizens of other States, and other parts of the United States, is unlawful, until such insurrection shall cease or has been suppressed; that all goods and chattels, wares and merchandise, coming from any of the said States, with the exceptions aforesaid, into other parts of the United States, without the special license and permission of the President, through the Secretary of the Treasury, or proceeding to any of said States, with the exceptions aforesaid, by land or by water, together with the vessel or vehicle conveying the same, or conveying persons to or from said States, with said exceptions, will be forfeited to the United States." (Dated August 16, 1861, II. p. .)

It will be observed that these portions of this statute and of this proclamation were addressed either to loyal localities and loyal *citizens*, or to disloyal localities and to disloyal *inhabitants*. Both persons and places are described. Did LeMore & Co. fall within either class of these persons? Were they either loyal citizens or disloyal inhabitants? There is no semblance of proof that they were. They were simply neutrals, both in fact and in law. Again, were these cottons obnoxious to the prohibitions of commercial intercourse between the loyal and disloyal sections? Were they seized *in transitu* between such sections? Not so. They were deposited on the bank of the Ouachita, and were in the peaceable and lawful possession of neutrals when they were forcibly seized. Hence, by no sort of construction can they be lawfully subjected to confiscation. Moreover, both the statute and the proclamation distinguish persons—calling those adhering to the Union *citizens*, and those adhering to the Confederate States *inhabitants*, thus conceding, at least by implication, that the latter were members of a hostile State, an implication carrying with it belligerent rights.

Another of these statutes, entitled "An Act to confiscate

property used for insurrectionary purposes," approved August 6, 1861, enacts, in its first section,

"That if, during the present rebellion, * * * any person or persons, his, her, or their agent, attorney or employee, shall purchase or acquire, sell or give, any property, of whatsoever kind or description, with intent to use or employ the same, or suffer the same to be used or employed, in aiding, abetting, or promoting such insurrection or resistance to the laws, or any person or persons engaged therein; or if any person or persons, being the owner or owners of any such property, shall knowingly use or employ, or consent to the use or employment, of the same, as aforesaid, all such property is hereby declared to be lawful subject of prize and capture wherever found; and it shall be the duty of the President of the United States to cause the same to be seized, confiscated, and condemned." (Vide U. S. Stats. at Large, vol. 12, p. 319.)

It has been contended by the law officers of the United States, and may be contended by others, that these cottons are obnoxious to the penalty provided by this act. This assumption proceeds upon these facts, viz: That LeMore & Co. purchased the cottons from Quegrouze, he from the Confederate Government, and it from John T. Simmons, in consideration of $50,000 paid in Confederate bonds. But this position is assailable on several grounds:

1st. Because neither the penalty prescribed by the act of July 13, nor that prescribed by the act of August 6, attaches to artificial, but only to natural persons. The former act expressly names "citizens" and "inhabitants" as the subjects of its operation. The latter, without being so explicit, names "persons," meaning unmistakably, in the sense of its context, natural persons. Both acts are in *pari materia*, and therefore ought, as respects the persons affected, as in all other points of similitude, to receive, according to established rules, a consistent and harmonious construction.

2d. Because both statutes were powerless to inflict penalties, either upon artificial or natural persons, actually withdrawn from their operation, and who were in fact amenable to an existing hostile jurisdiction. As to such persons both statutes were a mere *brutum fulmen;* as much so, as to the insurgents and the insurgent government, as to the subjects and government of the British empire.

3d. Because these cottons were exempted from the operation of these statutes, as of a local and municipal character, by the public law, unless it appears that they were obnoxious to certain exceptions made by that law.

Kent says that "the general usage now is not to touch private property upon land without making necessary compensation, unless in special cases, dictated by the necessary operations of war, or when captured in places carried by storm, and which repelled all overtures for a capitulation. Contributions are sometimes levied upon a conquered country in lieu of confiscation of property and as some indemnity for the expense of maintaining order and affording protection. If the conqueror goes beyond these limits wantonly, or when it is not clearly indispensable to the just purposes of war, and seizes private property of pacific persons for the sake of gain, * * * he violates the modern usages of war, and is sure to meet with indignant resentment, and to be held up to the general scorn and detestation of the world." (Kent's Com's., vol. 1, pp. 102, 103, 104, 10th edit. Vattel, b. 2, c. 8, sec. 147; c. 9, sec. 165.)

The exceptions here enumerated are few in number and very limited in their nature. Can it be said that the cottons in question fall within the terms or spirit of any of them? There is a total absence of proof and presumption to that effect. They were unquestionably not in any place carried by storm; nor was their seizure called for by any necessary operation of war; nor has any compensation been made for them. In no appreciable way could or did their seizure facilitate or retard the success of the Federal arms. Whether left or taken, as private property in the hands of neutrals, they could not add to or take from the resources of the enemy, who had received a consideration for them from a previous purchaser. Their spoliation was simply a wrong inflicted on a neutral and friend.

"Contributions," according to the authorities last cited, "are sometimes levied" upon a conquered country, in lieu of confiscations of property, and as some indemnity for the expense of maintaining order and affording protection." But even this condition as an authority for levying contributions did not exist in this case, for the country in which the cottons were seized was not conquered. The spoliation was the fruit of a hasty invasion, as hastily repelled by the disaster which befel the Federal arms at the "Sabine Cross Roads," and which immediately restored the Confederate jurisdiction over an extensive region, including the spot on which this act of spoliation was committed.

Therefore, in no sense, whether in virtue of conquest, or

of maintaining order or affording protection to the conquered, was the exaction of contributions, much less the spoliation of private property, authorized.

A third act has sometimes been referred to as legalizing this seizure: "An act to suppress insurrection, to punish treason and rebellion, to seize and confiscate the property of rebels, and for other purposes," approved July 17, 1862.

The sixth section of this act provides, "that if any person within any State or Territory of the United States, other than those (persons) named, as aforesaid, after the passage of this act, being engaged in armed rebellion against the Government of the United States, or aiding or abetting such rebellion, shall not, within sixty days after public warning and proclamation, duly given and made by the President of the United States, * * * all the estate and property, moneys, stocks, and credits of such person shall be liable to seizure as aforesaid, and it shall be the duty of the President to seize and use them as aforesaid, (for the support of the army,) or the proceeds thereof. And all sales, transfers, and conveyances, of any such property, after the expiration of sixty days from the date of such warning and proclamation, shall be null and void," &c.

Sec. 7. "That to secure the condemnation and sale of such property, after the same shall have been seized, * * * proceedings *in rem* shall be instituted in the name of the United States," &c. (U. S. Stats. at Large, vol. 12, p. 591.)

This is an extraordinary statute, perhaps without a parallel in the whole range of Christian legislation. It assumes nine millions of people, inhabiting the territory of eleven great States, both being almost entirely under the actual jurisdiction of a *de facto* government, to be absolutely amenable to another hostile authority. Is this assumption at all tenable? Is it not antagonistic to long-established principles and usage? It has been held in England that the statute of treason applies to a king *de facto* and not *de jure;* that a superior that has got possession of the throne is a king within the meaning of the statute, as there is a temporary allegiance due him for his administration of the government and temporary protection of the public, and, therefore, treasons so committed against Henry VI were punished under Edward IV, though all the line of Lancaster had been previously declared usurpers by act of parliament. And Hale carries the point of possession so far, that he holds a king out of possession is so far from having any right to our allegiance by any other title that he may set up against the king in being, that we are bound by the duty of our allegiance to resist him." (Hale's Pleas of the Crown, p. 104.)

"The true distinction, however, seems to be, that the statute of Henry VII does by no means command any opposition to a king *de jure*, but excuses the obedience paid to a king *de facto*. When, therefore, an usurper is in possession, the subject is excused in obeying and giving him assistance; otherwise, under an usurpation, no man would be safe, if the lawful prince had a right to hang him for obedience to the powers in being, as the usurper would certainly do so for disobedience." (Stephens's (Blackstone's) Commentaries on the Law of England, vol. 4, p. 221.)

Grotius says: "The acts of sovereignty which an usurper exercises, even before he has acquired an established right by long possession or convention, and while his possessory title is unjust, may be obligatory, not in virtue of his right, for he has none, but because there is every reason to suppose that the legitimate sovereign, whether people, king, or senate, would prefer that the usurper should be temporarily obeyed, than that the administration of the laws and justice should be interrupted, and the State exposed to all the disorders of anarchy." (De Jur. Bello ac Pac., lib. I, cap. 4, sec. 15.)

"Although there is a broad and obvious distinction between an insurrection of a conquered city or province against the conqueror and a revolution against an established government, yet it will be found on examination that both rest upon the same general principle—the relation of protection and allegiance, or the reciprocity of right and obligation." (Halleck Intern. Law, p. 792.)

"Neutrals are bound to take notice of the military right possession gives, and which is the only evidence of right acquired by military force, as contradistinguished from civil rights and titles. They are bound to take the *fact* for the *law*." (Kent's Com., vol. 1, p. 120.)

Returning, however, to the act of July 17, 1862, we find that it confounds the loyal with the disloyal, the innocent with the guilty, and subjects the property of both, as common enemies, to confiscation. Such is necessarily the effect, because every man who aided the rebellion, whether by contributing taxes, by service in the ranks, or in any civil or military post, or otherwise, although unwillingly, is made obnoxious to its penalties. Thus belligerent consequences are sought to be added to municipal punishment, and the subjects of both at the same treated as public enemies and private malefactors. Is this admissible? Is it not contrary to authority and natural justice? If, indeed, such persons are public enemies, they are, by the laws of war, excepted from the category of domestic traitors. If, on the other hand, some are traitors and others are loyal, a distinction should be drawn, and the one punished and the other spared by the municipal law.

In the case of civil war, it has been said by a justice of the Supreme Court of the United States, that "the citizens or subjects residing within the insurrectionary district, not implicated in the rebellion, but adhering to their allegiance, are not enemies, nor to be regarded as such. This distinction was constantly observed by the English government in the disturbances in Scotland under the Pretender and his son, in the years 1715 and 1745. It modifies the condition of the citizens or subjects residing in the limits of the revolted district who remain loyal to the government." (Justice Nelson's Charge to the Grand Jury, 2 Circuit, 1862.)

And it may be added, that this charge was given in view of the fact that many of the inhabitants within the Confederate limits, notwithstanding their actual situation, still remained loyal to the United States. And what evidence is there that Quegrouze, from whom LeMore & Co. derived their right to these cottons, was not a loyal citizen, although found within the Confederate limits?

The constitution of most, if not all, civilized countries, pronounce such penalties void. The Spanish constitution (article 10) provides that "the penalty of confiscation shall never be imposed." (Cas Gayon Diccionario de Derecho Administrativo Español, p. 360.)

The twelfth article of the constitution of Belgium declares that "the punishment of confiscation of property can never be established." (Code Civil Belgé, p. 2.)

The French charter of 1814 (article 66) declares that "the punishment by confiscation of property is abolished, and shall never be re-established." The fifty-seventh article of the constitution of August 14, 1830, is expressed in the same terms, as also the twelfth article of the constitution of 1848, which remains in force so far as it is not altered by the constitution of 7th (10) of November, 1852. (Tripiér Code Politique, pp. 244, 272, 319, 398.)

Another clause of the statute of July 17, 1865, provides that "all sales, transfers, or conveyances of any such property, after the expiration of the said sixty days, * * * * shall be null and void."

Understood in its plain and natural sense, what is the legal effect of this clause? In prohibiting the sale or purchase of bread, meat, raiment, and all the necessaries of life, as constituting part of the subjects of contract, it denounced the penalties of starvation against all whose condition required them to become vendors or purchasers of such articles. Is such an enactment valid? Is it not unprecedented? Will not the moral sense of the world repudiate it, not only in the respect mentioned, but in respect to all subjects of lawful trade? There can hardly be a doubt of it.

Again, is such an enactment legally capable to disturb the private relations existing between such persons, whatever their character as to loyalty or disloyalty? On this point Chief Justice Marshall (U. S.) says: "It may not be unworthy to remark, that it is very unusual, even in cases of conquest, for the conqueror to do more than to displace the sovereign and assume dominion over the country. The *modern usage* of nations, which has become *law*, would be violated; that sense of justice and of right, which is acknowledged and felt by the whole civilized world, would be outraged, if *private property* should be *generally confiscated* and *private rights annulled*. The people change their allegiance * * * , but *their relations* to each other, and their *private rights of property*, remain undisturbed." (Peters' Reports, vol. 7, page 86; United States *vs.* Percheman.)

The decisions of other American jurists go still further. The circuit court of the fifth circuit of Kentucky has declared that a private soldier of the rebel army may rely upon the belligerent rights conceded to the late so-called Confederacy as a defense in a civil suit for property taken according to the usages of war. The court adds: "Another view of the facts of this case tends to strengthen the conclusion that the rights and responsibilities of the defendant * * * must be determined by the laws of war regulating public wars between foreign States. The defendant, before the commencement of this war, was a citizen and resident of the State of Texas, and owed to that State a true and faithful allegiance, recognized by the fundamental laws of both State and Federal Government. This allegiance to his State, it is true, was subordinate to the allegiance which he owed to the Federal Government, which is supreme in its sphere; but it was nevertheless an allegiance properly owing to that State, which gave him protection for his life and property. * * * *

"Notwithstanding the State of Texas had by its ordinance

seceded from the Union, it was the duty of the defendant to adhere to the Federal Government, especially as there was no sufficient cause to justify the revolution. *But allegiance and protection are correlative terms or duties.*"

"And where the Federal Government, as is averred in this case, *did not* and could not, protect the defendant in refusing to submit to the civil and military power of the State of Texas, it surely would be unjust to exact from him the full and complete discharge of his allegiance and duties to the Federal Government, and deny him—especially in a State court—a defense based upon these rights, which the law of nations and of war confer upon the people of a *de facto* State in revolt against the established Government." (Am. Law Reg., Jan. 1866, vol. 4, No. 3, Hughes *vs.* Litsey, *et al.*, p. 148; U. S. *vs.* Rice, 4 Wheat.'s Reps., p. 254; U. S. *vs.* Hayward, 2 Gall. Rep., p. 500.)

Substituting the United States and LeMore & Co. as parties, for the preceding parties, this decision would be equally conclusive, at least with respect to the principles enunciated, with this advantage of facts in favor of LeMore & Co., that they were friends and neutrals; that neither Simmons nor Quegrouze are shown to have been armed rebels; and if the Confederate Government, an intermediate owner of the cottons, was, in fact, an offender, so were Litsey and his co-defendants.

So late as September, 1865, the Circuit Court of the fifth circuit of Arkansas decided that the rights and obligations of private contracts, entered into by private persons, although actually and constructively rebels, were not invalidated, but capable of being enforced, even by the loyal tribunals now established in that State. (Filkins *vs.* Hawkins, Am. Law Register, Jan., 1866, Vol. 4, No. 3.)

The fifth article of the Amendment to the Constitution of the United States provides that "no person shall * * * be deprived of life, liberty or property, without due process of law," &c.

Story says this clause is but an enlargement of the language of Magna Charta, "*nec super cum mittimus, nisi per legale judicium parium suorum vel per legem terræ;*" neither will he pass upon him or condemn him, but by the lawful judgment of his peers, or by the law of the land. Lord Coke says that these words, *per legem terræ*, mean by due process of law, that is, without due presentment or indictment, and being brought in to answer thereto by the due process of the common law. (Story's Com's on the Const. U. S., vol. 3, p. 661.)

Kent says "it may be received as a proposition, universally understood and acknowledged throughout this country, (U. S.,) that no person can be taken or imprisoned or disseized of his freehold or estate, or exiled or condemned, or deprived of life, liberty or property, unless by the law of the land or the judgment of his peers. The words by the law of the land, as used originally in *Magna Charta* in reference to this subject, are understood to mean due process of law, 'that is, by indictment or presentment of good and lawful men;' and this, says Lord Coke, is the true sense and exposition of these words. The latter and larger definition of *due process of law* is, that it means law in its regular course of administration, through the courts of justice." (Kent's Com's., vol. 1, pp. 623, 624, 625; Murray's Lessee *vs.* Hoboken L. & T. Co., 18 Howard's U. S., 272; Wynehamer *vs.* The People, 3 Kern, 378; People *vs.* Berberrich, 11 Howard Pr. Rep., 289.)

"The law of the land," in bills of right, Ch. J. Ruffin, in an elaborate opinion, says, "does not mean merely an *act of the legislature*, for that construction would *abrogate* all restrictions on legislative authority. The clause means, that statutes that would *deprive* a citizen of the rights of person or property, without a *regular trial, according to the course and usage* of the common law, would not be the law of the land in the sense of the Constitution." (Hoke *vs.* Henderson, 4 Dev. N. C. Rep. Justice Branson adopts the same construction, 4 Hill N. Y. Rep., pp. 146, 147.)

The courts in Tennessee have held that the terms "*the judgment of his peers*" means trial by a jury of twelve men, according to the *course* of the common law, and even in private suits at common law, the right of trial by jury is preserved in the Constitution of the United States, where the *value* in controversy exceeds twenty dollars." (Budd *vs.* The State, 3 Hump. Tenn. Rep., 483; Amendments Const. U. S., art. 7, sec. 2.)

"The United States cannot deprive a party of the right of trial by jury of issues of fact, by referring such issues to referees." (U. S. *vs.* Rathbone, 2 Paine, C. C., 578.)

What is the import of these authorities? What their bearing upon the present case? Clearly, that the United States cannot lawfully confiscate these cottons, except as a consequence of a previous trial and conviction of their owners. No legislative assumption as to the culpability, either of the cottons or their owners, can operate an avoidance of this prerequisite. No statutory artifice of a proceeding *in rem*, founded on such assumption, will avail for that purpose. Nor is such a proceeding competent upon the assumption that the cottons are, according to the public law, lawful *prize* or *spoil* of war, for they were not captured upon the high seas, or implicated in any act of hostility on land, or in any act violative of the law of contraband or of blockade.

But pursuing this line of argument still further, what is the language of the Constitution on this point? The last member of the first clause, of the 3d section, of the 3d article of that instrument, declares that "no person shall be convicted of treason, unless on the testimony of two witnesses to the same overt act," or on "confession in open court."

The second clause of the same section provides that "the Congress shall have power to declare the punishment of treason; but no attainder of treason shall work corruption of blood or forfeiture, except during the life of the person attainted.

And the 5th and 6th articles of the Amendments of that instrument, provide, among other things; that "no person shall be held, or answer for a capital or otherwise infamous crime, *unless* on presentment or indictment of a grand jury," &c. In all criminal prosecutions the accused shall enjoy the right of a speedy trial, by an impartial jury of the State and district wherein the crime shall have been committed, and to be informed of the nature and cause of the accusation; to have compulsory process for obtaining witnesses in his favor; and to have the assistance of counsel."

Now, has there been any conviction "of treason," in this cause, "on the testimony of two witnesses," or "on confession" of that offence? Has there been any "attainder of treason" or "forfeiture" as the consequence of such attainder? Have any of the successive owners of these cottons been "held to answer for a capital, or otherwise infamous crime," on presentment or indictment? Have any of them been permitted to "enjoy the right of" "trial by an impartial jury," or by any jury any where, for the crime supposed? Have they been "informed of the nature and cause of any accusation," "confronted with the witnesses against them," or had "compulsory process for obtaining witnesses in their favor." Not so. Not one of these conditions has been complied with. Not one of these sacred and inviolable muniments and safeguards thrown around the individual by the Constitution for his protection has been respected. On the contrary, they have been disregarded, and the subterfuge of a proceeding *in rem* to confiscation is substituted for the proceeding in *personam* to the same end. Is this not an overthrow of the Constitution in its vital properties; in its essential conditions? What survives of security for personal liberty or property rights under a usurpation so gross and complete? The hostile passions of the populace may justify or excuse it for the moment, but the sober and enlightened verdict of justice and posterity will repudiate it.

The coincidence of the common law of England with the Constitution of the United States but adds to the force of this argument. The common law of England is in force here as well as there; and it declares that "lands are forfeited upon *attainder*, and not *before;* goods and chattels are *forfeited by conviction*, because in many of the cases where goods are forfeited, there never is any attainder; which happens only where judgment of death or outlawry is given; therefore, in those cases the forfeiture must be upon conviction or not at all." (Chitty's Blackstone, vol. 2, b. 4, p. 287.)

Thus, under the common law of England, as under the Constitution of the United States, there can be no forfeiture without attainder or conviction, and there can be no conviction without previous indictment of the accused, his trial by his peers, and the strict observance of all other solemnities and forms required.

Aside from these explicit and peremptory texts, the United States are estopped by former political and judicial precedents established by themselves in analogous cases. Take the controversy between the United States and Peru, growing out of the capture and confiscation by the latter of two American vessels, for taking guano under the authority of some of the revolted provinces of Peru from certain seaports and guano deposits within those provinces, contrary to the laws of Peru. In this case the President of the United States (Mr. Buchanan) maintained that the citizens or subjects of a foreign nation may carry on trade with the portions of a country in the hands of either of the parties to a civil war, and without awaiting any action on the part of their own government; nor in *such* case can they be subjected to capture or detention by the *other* party, unless for the violation of neutral obligations.

He adds: "When a portion of one nation is taken possession of by the forces of another, with which it is at war, the conquering party has an undoubted right to declare the law of the place as long as this occupation continues, and all the rights of the previous sovereign are suspended until

3

his possession is resumed. It is equally well settled, that, when the former government resumes its possession of the territory, whether by force or under a treaty, it cannot call the citizens or subjects of a third nation to account for obeying the authority which was temporarily supreme during the enemy's occupation of the place.

The *jus postliminii* has no sort of application to such a case. When the people of a republic are divided into two hostile parties, who take up arms and oppose one another by military force, this is civil war. Supposing, however, that the rebellion is partially successful, and the old government maintains itself in one part of its territory, while it is obliged to surrender another, shall it then give law where it has no power to enforce obedience, or shall its authority be confined to the territory which it occupies? A revolutionary party, like a foreign belligerent power, is supreme over the country it conquers, as far and as long as its arms can maintain it." (Opinion of Mr. Black, Attorney General of the United States, May 15, 1858; Congressional Doc., 35th Cong., 1st Ses.; Senate Ex. Doc. No. 69, pp. 28, 29.)

In answer to the statement of the Peruvian Minister, it was said by Mr. Cass, U. S. Secretary of State: "Mr. Ozma insists that the existence or non-existence of civil war is a question not of fact, but of law, which no private person has a right to decide for himself. That foreigners must regard the former state of things still existing, unless their respective governments have recognized the change. I am clearly of the opinion that an American citizen who goes to Peru may safely act upon the evidence of his own senses. He has no choice. The government *de facto* will compel his obedience. If he resists the authority of the party in possession, on the ground that another has a right of possession, he departs from his neutrality, and so violates the duty he owes to both the belligerents as well as to the laws of his own country." (Mr. Cass to Mr. Clay, Minister to Peru, Nov. 26, 1858.)

What authority could be fuller or more definite on all points involved in the present controversy? Let us consider.

It is here mentioned, "that citizens or subjects of a *foreign* nation may carry on *commerce* with the *portions* of a country in the hands of either of the *parties* to a *civil* war, and *without* awaiting any action on the part of *their own* governments, *nor* in *such* case can they be *subjected* to *capture* or detention by the other party, unless for a violation of neutral obligations."

What more or less have LeMore & Co. done? Were they not the citizens of a foreign nation? Were they not carrying on trade with one of the parties to a civil war within a portion of country within its hands? Did they violate any neutral obligations? Can they be subjected to capture or detention; still less to confiscation? Surely not, consistently with the proofs they have adduced, and the reasoning and determination of the United States in the above case.

The authority of this case extends still further. It establishes the position that, upon the resumption by a government *de jure* of a territory temporarily wrested from it by insurrection, it cannot lawfully call the citizens or subjects of a *third* nation to account for obeying the authority which was temporarily supreme during the enemy's occupation. It asserts that the *jus postliminii* has no sort of application to such a case. The United States, therefore, having resumed possession of Louisiana, cannot, in virtue of that fact, lawfully call LeMore & Co., as citizens of a *third* nation, to answer for recognizing the hostile authority thus displaced. Nor can they, while claiming to be restored to their rights as they existed before the rebellion, lawfully claim to create new rights through the operation of legal penalties which were incapable of being enforced, and which, for that reason, were null when they were enacted. As the Attorney General has justly said, "can the government *de jure* give law where it has no power to enforce obedience." Could it give law to LeMore & Co., as neutrals, or to Simmons or Quegrouze, as actual or constructive rebels; or as loyal citizens locally subject to a revolutionary Power; or to that Power itself, which was for the time defiant and triumphant?

If, in fact, Simmons and Quegrouze had been loyal citizens domiciled in a loyal State, or in a loyal part of a disloyal State, the statute of July 13, 1861, prohibiting trade between such citizens, and such States or parts of States, and the inhabitants of the insurrectionary States, or of insurrectionary parts of States, would not have applied to them, under the circumstances; for by quitting their domicils and going into the enemy's jurisdiction, and sojourning and trading there without the President's license, they *ipso facto* violated their allegiance and became rebels in the eye of the public as well as the municipal law—taking all the rights and incurring all the responsibilities of that character. Even if they had gone into a neutral country, without competent license, during the war, they would have been offenders; much more so, going into, sojourning and trading in a belligerent country without such license.

In truth, Simmons was an inhabitant of Louisiana; there firmly domiciled; and as such, by force of recent adjudications, was, if not actually, at least constructively, a rebel.

The Supreme Court of the United States say "all persons residing within the territory occupied by the hostile party in this contest are liable to be treated as enemies, though not foreigners." (U. S. *vs.* Amy Warwick, on prize, 2 Black's Rep., p. 636.)

"It said, that though remaining in the rebel territory, Mrs. Alexander has no personal sympathy with the rebel cause, and that her property, therefore, cannot be regarded as enemy's property; but this Court cannot inquire into the personal character and dispositions of individual inhabitants of every territory. We must be governed by the principle of public law, so often announced from this bench as applicable alike to civil and international wars, that all the people of each State or district in insurrection against the United States must be regarded as enemies until, by the action of the legislative and the executive, or otherwise, that relation is thoroughly and permanently changed." (Mrs. Alexander's cotton, 2 Wallace, p. 419.)

The pertinency of the reasoning of the Court in these cases will appear by reference to certain facts. Quegrouze (although it does not appear in the evidence) had been a rebel officer, wounded in the battle of Shiloh, and returned in consequence to his home in New Orleans, where he was registered by the Federal authorities as a rebel, and whence he was banished, because he would not take an oath of allegiance to the United States. He left New Orleans as a refugee in November, 1862, and on the 14th of July, 1865, after the failure of the rebellion, took the required oath of allegiance, styling himself "a citizen of Louisiana, C. S." In August of the same year, after an absence of nearly three years, he returned to New Orleans.

Thus, in every possible view, the political *status* of Simmons and Quegrouze, places them beyond the Federal jurisdiction, exempted them from the commercial disabilities attaching to loyal citizens under the municipal law, and clothed them with the capacity to receive and transmit title under the laws of nations.

In 1817 certain Spanish American provinces revolted against the Spanish crown, and, under the title of United Provinces of "*Rio de la Plata,*" proclaimed their independence, and resorted to war to maintain it. During the war two Spanish vessels, carrying nine bales of cochineal, two bales of jalap, and one box of vanilla, belonging to Spanish subjects, were captured by the naval force of the revolutionary government. These goods were taken on board of the capturing vessels and brought into the port of Norfolk, Virginia, as prize of war. Whilst there they were libelled in the United States District Court of that State by the Spanish consul in behalf of their original Spanish owners, and sentence was passed. An appeal was taken to the Supreme Court of the United States, and, on the hearing of the appeal, it was held that "the Government of the United States recognized the existence of civil war between Spain and her colonies, and has avowed a determination to remain neutral between the parties, and to allow to each the same rights of asylum and hospitality and intercourse. Each party is, therefore, deemed by us as a belligerent nation, having, so far as concerns us, the same sovereign rights of war, and entitled to be respected in the exercise of these rights. We cannot interfere to the prejudice of either belligerent without making ourselves a party to the contest, and departing from the posture of neutrality. All captures made by each must be considered as having the same validity," &c. (7 Wheaton, pp. 284, 5, 6.)

The parity of this case with that of LeMore & Co., in all the essential qualities of both, is most striking. The United States was a neutral in one case, allowed the same rights of intercourse and of war, and the same validity to the captures of each of the belligerents. France was a neutral in the other, and did the same thing; recognizing the same right of a rebel to buy and sell that was freely attributed to a loyalist.

With what right or justice, therefore, can the United States claim at this time to confiscate property sold by a rebel to a neutral? With what consistency can it, as a party to a civil war, repudiate its own former solemn political and judicial decisions in a parallel case, in which it was no party? Can it do so because it would lose in the one case what it would gain in the other? Who will say so?

Moreover, the doctrine of institutional writers, no less than the custom of civilized nations. exempts certain persons from the direct effect of military operations; these persons are the sovereign and his family, the members of the civil government, women and children, cultivators of the soil, artisans, laborers, merchants, men of science and letters, and generally all other public or private persons engaged in the ordinary civil pursuits of life, unless *actually* taken *in* arms, or guilty of some other misconduct violative of the usages of war, by which they forfeit their immunity." (Lawrence's Wheaton Intern. L., pp. 593, 594, 595, 596.

Are not Simmons, Quegrouze and LeMore & Co. exempted by the operation of this rule? Were they, or either of them, actually taken in arms or guilty of any misconduct violative of the usages of war? Had they, either as inhabitants of the Confederate States or as neutrals, forfeited these immunities? It will scarcely be so regarded in the face of facts and the authority here cited.

Next: What are the legal consequences of the peace which has followed the overthrow of the rebellion? Are the vanquished to be regarded as a subjugated people, and the victors as conquerors? This would imply that the war had been waged for conquest between foreign nations, which is not true. As we have seen, it was a civil war—a war between members of the same State, waged on the one side to establish a separate nationality; on the other to maintain an undivided one. The object of the victors was not to gain a new title, but to retain an old one; to re-establish their superiority where it had been displaced; to preserve the Union, not to destroy it.

It is true that conquest carries with it absolute and unlimited sovereign rights over the conquered country, but no nation ever makes such a conquest over its own territory. No heresy could be more dangerous and deplorable than the supposition that such rights have inured to the United States as a consequence of the suppression of the late rebellion, and that both the States and the people over whom their arms have prevailed, have no longer any political rights or existence. Such a doctrine would be but an aggravation of rebellion, the legalization and confirmation of disunion.

Peace having supervened, belligerent rights can no longer be exercised, simply because these are no longer belligerents. The public law ceases to operate, and the right which it gives to proceed *in rem*, except as to offending property, ceases with it. The municipal law now takes its place, and under it there can be no confiscation of property, under the limitations imposed by the Federal Constitution, except incidentally to the conviction of its owner, in the manner prescribed by that instrument. In short, confiscation, except of offending property, as one of the means provided by municipal law to put an end to the rebellion, ceases with the rebellion itself.

It only remains to inquire how far the sentence of the

judicial tribunals of the United States is binding upon the parties to this controversy. It is binding on the captors as citizens of the United States, because these tribunals have a competent jurisdiction over their persons. But Le-More & Co. are not bound to submit to it, as citizens of France, because the tribunals pronouncing it have no jurisdiction over them, either in respect to their persons or the goods in controversy. Hence, if justice is not done to them, they may apply to their own sovereign for a remedy, who may, consistently with the law of nations, give them a remedy either by solemn war or reprisals. The King of Prussia, in 1753, acted on this well established right, and made reprisals by stopping the interest upon a loan due to British subjects, and secured by hypothecation upon the revenues of Silesia, until he actually obtained from the British Government an indemnity for certain vessels unjustly captured from Prussian subjects by the British navy, and condemned by the British Admiralty. (Vattel, Droit des Gens, liv. 2, ch. 7, s. 84; Wheaton's Hist. Law of Nat., pp. 206–217.)

So, also, under the treaty of 1794, between the United States and Great Britain, a mixed commission was appointed to determine the claims of American citizens, arising from the capture of their property by British cruisers during the then existing war with France, acording to justice, equity and the law of nations. In the course of the proceedings of this board, objections were made by the British Government against the commissioners proceeding to hear and determine any case where sentence of condemnation had been affirmed by the Lords of Appeal in prize causes, upon the ground that full and entire credit was to be given to their sentence, inasmuch as, according to the general law of nations, it was to be presumed that justice had been administered by this, the competent and supreme tribunal in matters of prize. But this objection was overruled by the board, upon the grounds and principles already stated, and a full and satisfactory indemnity was awarded in many causes where there had been a final sentence of condemnation. (Lawrence's Wheaton's Intern. L., pp. 679, 680.)

JOHN A. McCLERNAND.

For McCLERNAND, BROADWELL & SPRINGER,
Attorneys and Counsellors at Law.

www.ingramcontent.com/pod-product-compliance
Lightning Source LLC
LaVergne TN
LVHW011141110826
845150LV00008B/2444

* 9 7 8 1 4 1 8 1 9 3 3 7 9 *